Young Heroes

Emmanuel Ofosu Yeboah

Champion for Ghana's Disabled

Leanne K. Currie-McGhee

KIDHAVEN PRESS

An imprint of Thomson Gale, a part of The Thomson Corporation

Detroit • New York • San Diego • San Francisco
Boston • New Haven, Conn. • Waterville, Maine
London • Munich

THOMSON

GALE

™

LIBRARY OF CONGRESS CATALOGING-IN-PUBLICATION DATA

Currie-McGhee, L. K. (Leanne K.)
Emmanuel Ofosu Yeboah: champion for Ghana's disabled / by Leanne K. Currie-McGhee.
p. cm. — (Young heroes)
Includes bibliographical references and index.
ISBN 0-7377-3614-3 (hard cover : alk. paper) 1. Yeboah, Emmanuel Ofosu, 1977–2. People with disabilities—Ghana—Biography—Juvenile literature. 3. People with disabilities—Ghana—Attitudes—Juvenile literature. 4. Public opinion—Ghana—Juvenile literature. 5. Ghana—Biography—Juvenile literature. I. Title. II. Series.
HV3013.Y43C87 2006
362.4'3092—dc22
                                                            2006009291

Printed in the United States of America

Contents

Introducing Emmanuel Ofosu Yeboah

In 2001 Emmanuel Ofosu Yeboah did something incredible. With just one leg, he rode a bike 370 miles (595km) around his home country, Ghana. Yeboah rode across the country to change able-bodied Ghanaians' view that **disabled** people are incapable of great achievements. This ride made Ghanaians reconsider their stereotype of disabled people. The ride also was Yeboah's first action as a disabled-rights activist.

When Emmanuel Yeboah was born in Ghana, no one expected him to ride a bike. No one expected him even to go to school. What people expected was that Yeboah would one day beg for a living. This is because Yeboah was born with a deformed right leg. In Ghana, most disabled people must beg to survive.

Fortunately for Yeboah, his mother had high expectations for him. Yeboah's mother sent him to school, despite the fact that most disabled Ghanaians were hidden

Emmanuel Yeboah, disabled from birth, has never let his disability keep him from achieving his goals.

at home. She told him never to let his disability get in the way of his dreams.

Yeboah's dream is to provide a better life for Ghana's disabled people. He wants all of Ghana's disabled citizens to have the opportunity to get an education, play sports, and receive job training. Yeboah bikes, speaks, and fundraises around the world to achieve his dream. Since the **documentary** that stars Yeboah, *Emmanuel's Gift,* first aired, he has become a well-known disabled-rights activist. "I see how people are treated in Ghana, and that's why I am giving all my effort to this,"[1] says Yeboah of his dream.

Chapter One

A Difficult Start

Most people celebrate when babies are born, but there was little celebration on May 5, 1977. On this day, Comfort Yeboah gave birth to Emmanuel Ofosu Yeboah in Koforidua, Ghana. People did not celebrate Emmanuel's birth, because he was physically disabled. Emmanuel did not have a lower right leg. His foot stuck out from behind his knee. This left him unable to learn to walk. In Ghana, the disabled are widely regarded as a burden to their families.

Emmanuel's father, Dickson Kwadjo Ofosu, abandoned Emmanuel and the rest of the family when he realized that Emmanuel was disabled. He thought Emmanuel's life would be worthless. People suggested that Emmanuel's mother poison her son or leave him by the edge of the river to die. This practice, known as "seeing off," is not uncommon in Ghana. "But Mommy didn't do that," says Yeboah. "She took very good care of me."[2]

Emmanuel's mother took him to doctors in an attempt to correct his deformed leg. The doctors told her that the leg could not be fixed. Although saddened that her son was physically disabled, Comfort Yeboah raised her son with love. She taught him that he deserved the right to the same treatment as able-bodied Ghanaians.

Obstacles to Overcome

Emmanuel's mother believed that he deserved an education, even though she knew that it would be difficult. The Yeboah family was very poor. Emmanuel grew up in a home that did not have electricity or plumbing. The entire family, which included a younger brother and sister and other relatives, slept on a dirt floor. There was little money for school fees and supplies.

Another problem was Ghanaians' prejudice against the disabled. Ghanaian parents were discouraged from sending disabled children to school. Many schools would not even accept disabled children.

Emmanuel's mother overcame these obstacles. She sold vegetables in the local marketplace every day. She made enough money to take care of the family and send Emmanuel to school. Also, she did not let others' prejudice get in her way. She enrolled Emmanuel in the village school and paid no attention to those who suggested keeping him home.

Being Independent

As he grew up, Emmanuel continued to endure hardships. The village school was 2 miles (3.2km) from his home. Emmanuel could not walk, and his family could not af-

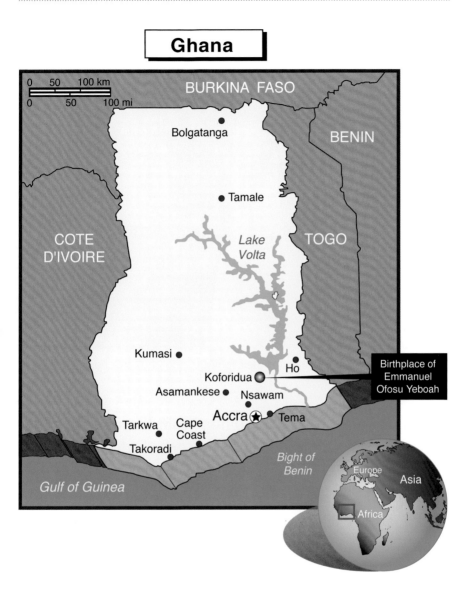

ford a wheelchair. So his mother carried him 2 miles to school and 2 miles home each day. As he grew older, Emmanuel was determined to get to and from school on his own. "I would hop on my leg,"[3] Emmanuel says.

Throughout his childhood, Emmanuel proved to others, including his own family, that he could do whatever

Ghanaian children fetch water for their families, one of many chores they are expected to do.

he set his mind to. "I had no hope that Emmanuel would walk, but with time he started to crawl, then hop, then jump and stand with help," says Emmanuel's grandmother. "This inspired me to give him an improvised walking stick."[4] Emmanuel learned to use this stick to walk with one leg.

Many people in Emmanuel's family felt he was unable to perform hard tasks. Emmanuel proved them wrong. He taught himself to fetch water and climb coconut trees just as well as able-bodied children.

Changing Opinions

Emmanuel also had to overcome the other students' prejudices against him. Of the 240 children in the village school, Emmanuel was the only disabled student. Although he went to school and church with them, many of the students ignored him. Other students teased him. Few children would play with him.

Emmanuel loved sports. He longed to play soccer with his classmates. He taught himself to play by hopping with his crutches. Still, the students refused to let him join the team.

Emmanuel grew tired of watching his classmates play without him. He decided to persuade them to let him play. He knew that few of the students owned their own soccer ball. Emmanuel earned pocket money working for a local shoemaker. He used the money to buy a soccer ball. He told his classmates that they could use the ball, but only if they included him on the team. They agreed to his terms, and Emmanuel got to play.

In order to find better employment, Yeboah journeyed to Accra, Ghana's capital (pictured).

Off to Accra

Emmanuel continued to attend school until he turned thirteen, but then his mother grew ill. After four operations on her stomach, she could not work. The family needed money for food and to pay her hospital bills. Emmanuel decided to take care of the family himself.

Emmanuel already earned a dollar a day as he shined shoes in the morning before school. He decided he needed to do more. Against his mother's wishes, Emmanuel quit school in order to find full-time work.

Emmanuel decided to look for a job shining shoes in Accra, Ghana's capital. He packed his crutches, tools to shine shoes, and a box to sit on. In the middle of the night, on his own, Emmanuel Yeboah began the 150-mile journey (241km) to Accra.

Ride of His Life

Emmanuel Yeboah knew no one in Accra, a city of about 2 million people. Once there, he met several disabled people and witnessed how difficult their lives were. Thousands of handicapped people begged on Accra's streets. He later learned that as many as 2 million people, about ten percent of Ghana's population, are disabled, and most beg for a living.

Yeboah learned that many of Ghana's disabled people were treated poorly. He watched people taunt, ignore, or, at best, throw coins to the disabled who lay on the streets. The reason for this treatment is that most Ghanaians believe a disabled person is a punishment to his or her family for something the family has done in the past.

Because of this belief, disabled Ghanaian babies may be poisoned or abandoned at birth. Other families hide their disabled children so that no one learns of their **handicaps.** Many disabled people are thrown out of their homes and forced to live on the streets.

Without money for a wheelchair, a polio sufferer in Africa is forced to crawl along the ground.

Making a Living

The disabled people Yeboah met could not work because they were not trained or educated. Also, many were not mobile enough to work. Ghana does not have enough wheelchairs and artificial limbs, or **prostheses**, for its disabled citizens. Few of the disabled can afford the equipment that is available.

For these reasons, the only way for many disabled people to survive is to beg. Those who beg can earn up to ten dollars a day. Yeboah did not consider this option. He earned two dollars a day shining 30 to 40 pairs of shoes.

When his mother grew sicker, Yeboah returned home with money to help the family. However, when he left Accra he did not forget what he had seen there. He came home with a determination to change the way people in Ghana view and treat the disabled.

A Vow

Soon after Yeboah returned to his village, his mother's health deteriorated. On Christmas Eve of 1997, she died at age 37. She gave Yeboah advice the night before her death. Comfort Yeboah told her son, "Don't let anybody put you down because of your disability."[5]

After she died, Yeboah felt a desire to share what his mother had taught him. "What my mother told me was a gift," he says. "I want to show everyone that physically

An African beggar with no hands and only one leg depends on the kindness of strangers.

A disabled man is helped to a voting booth in Accra.

challenged people can do something."[6] He vowed to show Ghana's people that disability does not mean inability. Because he enjoyed sports, Yeboah chose to ride a bike more than 370 miles (595km) across Ghana. He wanted to demonstrate what he could do, even with a deformed leg.

Many people, even Yeboah's friends, did not think he could accomplish his goal. For one thing, Yeboah did not have a prosthetic leg, so he would have to ride with just one leg. There was another major obstacle. Yeboah did not own a bike.

Getting a Bike

Yeboah could not afford a bike on his own. He asked companies in Ghana to sponsor his ride and donate a bike. The companies all said no. They did not believe he could accomplish his goal.

Then, something wonderful happened. Yeboah learned about the Challenged Athletes Foundation (CAF). This organization, based in California, helps people with physical disabilities participate in physical fitness and competitive athletics. In 2001 Yeboah wrote CAF a letter. He told them that his goal was to change Ghana's views of disabled people, and he needed a bike to do that. Yeboah prayed to God that he would receive good results from his letter.

Bob Babbitt, cofounder of CAF, read Yeboah's letter with amazement. "What impressed me from the very beginning about Emmanuel is that what he said in his note was not 'I'm a poor kid from Ghana and I've got a deformed leg, please send me money.' It was 'Send me a bicycle because I want to help other people. I want to prove a stereotype wrong.'"[7]

Babbitt decided not only to send Yeboah a bike, but CAF also donated a bike helmet, shorts, socks, and gloves. Yeboah was excited when he received the donation. He planned his route through the country, then talked to village chiefs and government officials so that they would know when he would be in their villages.

The Pozo

Since Yeboah could not use his right leg, he trained himself to ride a bike one-legged. People from the Disabled Society of Ghana helped coach him. He learned to pedal with his healthy left leg while his right foot rested on the bike's frame.

In September 2001 Yeboah began his ten-day, ten-night ride. He wore a red, yellow, and blue striped shirt that said "The Pozo." *Pozo* is Ghanaian slang for a disabled person who is doing something great. Yeboah wanted everyone who saw him to know that a disabled person was on the bike.

When his friends and his coworkers saw Yeboah ride on his bike, they gave him a big ovation. Newspapers and radio stations reported on Yeboah's progress. Yeboah rolled through village after village while children cheered and chased behind him. Throughout the journey, Yeboah stopped to deliver his message to government officials, ministers, and the media. He told

With strength and determination, Yeboah set out to prove that disabled people are capable of great achievements.

A crowd of children watches as Yeboah begins his bike ride across Ghana to challenge the idea of what it means to be disabled.

them that disabled people are capable of great accomplishments, and Ghana must improve its treatment of them.

By the end of the journey, Yeboah had won over many fans. He started his country talking about the disabled. Politicians began to understand they could not ignore the situation anymore. "I feel like I've achieved a lot not only for me but for my entire country," says Yeboah about his feelings immediately after the ride. "It makes me feel strong and happy and I want to ride and ride."[8]

Three

A Vision

Emmanuel Yeboah, who turned twenty-five in 2002, has a grand vision for Ghana. He wants able-bodied Ghanaians to respect the disabled. He wants to educate Ghana's disabled citizens so that they can get jobs. He wants to give Ghana's disabled citizens confidence through sports opportunities. His ride was the first step toward making the vision a reality.

In November 2002 the CAF helped him take the next step toward making his dreams for Ghana come true. The group offered to fly Yeboah to California to ride in the San Diego Triathlon Challenge, a fund-raiser that helps CAF provide athletic opportunities to people with physical disabilities.

Yeboah arrived in California with a suitcase and just three dollars in his pocket. CAF took care of Yeboah's room and board and helped him prepare for the race. During the race, he biked for seven hours using just one leg to finish the 56 miles (90km) of the triathlon's bike portion. "I did not realize San Diego was so hilly,"[9] Yeboah joked afterward.

An Opportunity

Yeboah got a surprise after he biked in the triathlon. One of the event sponsors, Loma Linda Hospital and Rehabilitation Center, offered him a prosthetic leg and the surgery he needed in order to wear it. Yeboah did not immediately say yes.

Yeboah is the main provider for his extended family in Ghana. He worried about who would care for them in his absence. The Loma Linda staff asked Yeboah what he needed to support his family. When he replied that he made two to three dollars a day in Ghana, the staff gave

Yeboah, actor David James Elliott (center), and CAF cofounder Bob Babbitt pose together at the 2003 San Diego Triathlon Challenge.

Just six weeks after receiving his prosthetic leg, Yeboah competes in a mini-triathlon.

him enough money to support his family for the three months he would need for surgery and recovery.

Yeboah also worried about the surgery. The doctors needed to **amputate** part of his deformed leg so that he could wear a prosthesis. In Ghana, people who undergo amputations often do not live. If they do live, they get useless prostheses after the amputation.

Getting a Leg

Fourteen-year-old Rudy Garcia-Tolson, a double amputee from Bloomington, California, befriended Yeboah. He assured Yeboah that if he got the surgery, he would be able to walk with a prosthetic leg. After Yeboah watched Garcia-Tolson excel in sports while wearing his two prosthetic legs, Yeboah decided to get the surgery.

In April 2003 Yeboah underwent the amputation. Just six weeks after the surgery, he did more than walk. With his new prosthetic leg, he ran, biked, and swam in Garcia-Tolson's Braveheart mini-triathlon. This event raises public awareness and funds for Loma Linda's outreach services for the physically challenged. Yeboah said he did the race to inspire others.

Three months after getting his prosthetic leg, Yeboah returned home. Although he could have stayed in the United States and enjoyed his new leg, Yeboah wanted to continue his work in Ghana. According to Bob Babbitt, Yeboah's attitude is, "You take care of me, I am going to take care of thousands more just like me."[10]

Back in Ghana

Yeboah returned to Ghana in the summer of 2003 with the same mission, but his new leg gave him more confidence. "I stood in the mirror, looked at myself and thought 'I can't believe it,'" Yeboah says. "I was like a new person. I was changed forever."[11] Yeboah bounded off the plane with his new leg and a clear vision for Ghana.

Yeboah's village chief organized a ceremony to celebrate Yeboah's achievements. The fact that Yeboah, a disabled person, received such an honor demonstrated how much he had already changed attitudes in Ghana. At the ceremony, Yeboah told people that in America he did not see disabled people begging on the streets. Yeboah asked for all Ghanaians to work together to get the disabled off the streets in Ghana.

Even Yeboah's father, Dickson Kwadjo Ofosu, whom Yeboah had not seen since birth, heard Yeboah's message. After Ofosu heard about Yeboah's achievements on the radio, he showed up in Koforidua to make amends. "Although he never took care of me, I have forgiven my father because my message is about bringing people together,"[12] Yeboah says.

Awards in America

Americans, like Ghanaians, wanted to honor Yeboah's efforts. CAF flew Yeboah back to the United States in November 2003 to receive CAF's Most Inspirational Athlete award. Actor Robin Williams, who volunteers with CAF, presented the award to Yeboah.

While in California for the awards ceremony, Yeboah again competed in CAF's annual San Diego Triathlon Challenge. With two legs, Yeboah shaved three hours off his 2002 race time. After the race, Yeboah flew to New York City. He met with fellow Ghanaian Kofi Anan, the secretary general of the

Yeboah rides in the cycling portion of a mini-triathlon before returning to Ghana.

United Nations, to discuss the rights of the disabled in Ghana. Anan told Yeboah that he should be proud of his efforts and continue them.

Yeboah then flew to Oregon to receive the 2003 Casey Martin Award from Nike Corporation. Nike gives this award to people who excel in sports while overcoming physical, mental, or societal challenges. Many of these people also speak out on behalf of other athletes with disabilities. Along with that award came a $25,000 grant. CAF matched the grant to help support Yeboah's mission in Ghana.

Emmanuel Yeboah's Vision

With the grant money in hand, Yeboah worked with CAF to develop specific goals to achieve his vision for Ghana's disabled citizens. He established Emmanuel's Fund and a detailed plan to use the fund to provide education, mobility, and sports opportunities for the disabled in Ghana. Specifically, he decided to provide scholarships to disabled Ghanaian children, wheelchairs to those in need, and sports equipment to the Disabled Sports Society of Ghana.

With a fund and plan in place, Yeboah immediately got to work. With help from both CAF and Ghana officials and organizations, he returned to Ghana near the end of 2003. He was ready to begin.

Chapter Four

Realizing the Dream

Once Yeboah established Emmanuel's Fund, he set out to use it. He decided to award scholarships annually to fifteen disabled students so that they could attend their village schools. The first fifteen students received their scholarships on March 26, 2004, at the king's palace in Kyebi.

Traditionally, the disabled were not allowed to enter Ghana's royal palaces, because people believed the disabled would bring a curse to the palace. Yeboah changed the thinking of King Osagyefuo, ruler of 2.5 million people in the eastern region of Ghana. On the day of the ceremony, the king proudly stood next to Yeboah as they gave out the scholarships.

Because he hosted the event at his palace, the king made a groundbreaking statement of support to the disabled community. The king further showed his support with his remarks. "[The disabled] may not walk like you and I

Yeboah's activism has helped disabled people gain more equality in Ghana.

walk, but they have a brain just like you and I. Poverty and disability must not be a bar to learning and education,"[13] King Osagyefuo stated.

Getting People Mobile

Yeboah also uses his fund and other donations to provide mobility to the disabled. An organization called Free Wheelchair Mission heard about Yeboah and donated wheelchairs to Ghana. Yeboah and others gave disabled Ghanaians 250 wheelchairs in March 2004.

A Free Wheelchair Mission board member and volunteer accompanied Yeboah as he distributed the wheelchairs. The first 100 chairs were presented in Koforidua, Yeboah's hometown. Over four hundred people sat patiently, with most of them arriving four hours before the ceremony. "As always, the rewards of seeing the disabled crawl across the ground and in an instant be granted mobility with their new chair are beyond comprehension," writes a representative from the Free Wheelchair Mission. "So is the disappointment of knowing hundreds and thousands never made it to the ceremony and still need mobility."[14]

Because he knew that thousands more disabled Ghanaians still needed wheelchairs, Yeboah enlisted King Osagyefuo's support. King Osagyefuo agreed to go with Yeboah to the United States. With Yeboah at his side, the king spoke at a Free Wheelchair Mission fund-raiser. His keynote address led to the donation of 500 wheelchairs for Ghana's handicapped people. Their visit to the United States also led to the donation of 50 prosthetic feet and adapter kits from Ossur, a company that makes prosthetics.

Starting a Movement

In addition to providing the disabled with mobility, Yeboah's efforts are getting them more respect. King Osagyefuo's support has played a major role in the change in Ghana's treatment of the disabled. With his speeches to Ghanaians and support of Yeboah's events, the king shows able-bodied Ghanaians that it is not right to shun the disabled. More Ghanaians now see the disabled as productive members of society.

Yeboah also works to change disabled persons' view of themselves. He shows them what he, a disabled person, is capable of accomplishing. Yeboah has convinced them that they are able to make a difference in how Ghana's disabled are treated. In 2004 inspired by Yeboah's accomplishments, six hundred fellow disabled took to Ghana's streets to protest for more rights. They asked the government to provide them with more educational and vocational opportunities so that they can support themselves.

Sports Opportunities

Yeboah also works to create opportunities in sports for Ghana's disabled citizens. He believes that sports empower disabled people. At the same ceremony that Yeboah and the king distributed scholarships, they also gave sports wheelchairs to five disabled athletes. These wheelchairs allow handicapped athletes to play basketball and take part in wheelchair races.

To provide more opportunities for the disabled to play sports, Yeboah has started a cycling team, a wheelchair basketball team, and a running team for physically challenged athletes. He also uses his fund to provide equipment for his sports teams and the athletes who play with the Disabled Sports Society of Ghana.

Yeboah has also taken steps to provide Ghana's disabled athletes a place to play wheelchair basketball, soccer, rugby, wheelchair racing, and more. A plan to build a sports academy is in the works. King Osagyefuo's tribe donated land for the sports academy, and Yeboah works to get more funds for building the academy.

Personal Life

Because of his perseverance, Yeboah fulfills dreams both for Ghana's disabled and for himself. He has become an athlete, something he longed for as a child. Yeboah races in events around the world.

Yeboah is so respected as an athlete that he was honored by the 2004 Organizing Committee for the Olympic Games. The committee selected Yeboah to represent Ghana as a torchbearer during the Olympic

Torch Relay. He took part in this historic event on June 11, 2004, in Giza, Egypt.

Yeboah has also realized his personal dream of being a husband and father. In 2003 after he received his prosthetic leg, Yeboah returned to Ghana ready to marry his love, Elizabeth, an able-bodied woman. At the time, a disabled person marrying an able-bodied person was unheard of in Ghana. This view did not stop Yeboah. He asked and received permission from Elizabeth's father to marry her in 2003. Then, on July 17, 2004, their daughter Linda, whom they named after the Loma Linda Hospital and Rehabilitation Center, was born. Emmanuel Yeboah now has great dreams for

Believing that sports enable disabled people, Yeboah works to bring sports opportunities like this one in a Kenyan refugee camp to Ghana's disabled citizens.

Yeboah has become a respected athlete as well as a champion of disabled rights.

his daughter and believes that she can do anything, just as his mother believed in him. "I will help her to achieve more than I have," he says. "I can see that my daughter is very brilliant and I am sure that my dreams about her will come true."[15]

Chapter Five

Emmanuel's Gift

When Emmanuel Yeboah fulfills one goal, he makes another goal. It is because of this unique trait that Yeboah has become the subject of a documentary film. Filmmakers Lisa Lax and Nancy Stern heard about Yeboah's story from Bob Babbitt, CAF cofounder. They were impressed with Yeboah's drive and vision. They wanted people to see his dedication to make the world a better place. Lax and Stern decided to film a documentary entitled *Emmanuel's Gift*.

Influential people became involved in the film's production. Oprah Winfrey, inspired by Yeboah, agreed to narrate the film. "I think every parent with a child able to go to the movies should take their children to see this movie. It will change the way your children think about what they can do and can be,"[16] Winfrey says.

Emmanuel's Gift premiered on February 4, 2005, at the Santa Barbara Film Festival in California. It played throughout the United States and became available on DVD. Since then, Yeboah has become well-known and appears on shows such as *CNN Live Today*, *The Oprah Winfrey Show*, and *The Today Show*.

Publicity Results

Yeboah uses his newfound fame to accomplish his mission. He encourages people to donate to his fund and organizations such as CAF and Free Wheelchair Mission. This allows him to provide additional wheelchairs to the disabled, educate more of Ghana's disabled children, and make strides toward opening a sports academy for the disabled.

Standing in front of a movie poster for *Emmanuel's Gift*, Yeboah attends a screening of the film about his life.

Emmanuel's Gift also has enabled Yeboah to become an influential **activist** for the disabled. He is able to get his message to powerful people. United Nations secretary general Kofi Anan, U.S. president George W. Bush, and Ghana's president Kuofor have met with Yeboah to honor his work.

34

Yeboah greets fans at the premiere of *Emmanuel's Gift.*

Arthur Ashe Courage Award

Politicians are not the only ones who have honored Yeboah. He received the **Arthur Ashe Courage Award** on July 17, 2005. This award honors athletes who contribute to society in areas that go far beyond sports. It is named for Arthur Ashe, the great African American tennis champion who fought racism and, after becoming sick with AIDS, also helped focus public attention on AIDS.

Actor Matthew Perry hosted the award ceremony, and Oprah Winfrey presented the award to both Emmanuel Yeboah and Jim MacLaren. MacLaren lost a leg at age twenty-two when a bus hit him. He came back from the accident to become a top marathon runner. Eight years after the first accident, he was struck by a van during a race. Today he has only partial use of his limbs but he travels the country speaking about overcoming difficult challenges in life.

Athletes Jim MacLaren and Emmanuel Yeboah pose for photographers before accepting the Arthur Ashe Courage Award.

Yeboah's and MacLaren's impact on people was easy to see at the ceremony. Major sports figures such as Bill Walton, Curt Schilling, Dwayne Wade, and Peyton Manning were moved to tears as Yeboah and MacLaren received the award. After they received the award, the audience gave the two men a long-standing ovation. Upon returning to Ghana, Yeboah presented the award to King Osagyefuo to show his appreciation for the king's support of his mission.

More to Do

Because he has made many friends in the United States, Yeboah could have chosen to remain in the country after the film's premiere. In the United States, Yeboah enjoys greater rights and respect than disabled citizens receive in Ghana. Yet Yeboah chose to return to Ghana. When asked why, Yeboah says, "It's something in my heart that I wanted to do to help my people. I wanted to come back to Ghana to support the disabled people here."[17] Yeboah has a long list of items to accomplish in Ghana.

One item on his list is to get Ghana involved in the Paralympic Games. This is a major sports competition for disabled athletes. He has organized a wheelchair basketball team that will represent Ghana at the 2008 games.

Another major focus of Yeboah's is to push Ghana's government to pass a national disability bill. The bill would ensure that all public places are wheelchair accessible, provide free education for persons with disability, and provide vocational training for people with disability. Several government officials, including Ghana's president Kuofor and king Osagyefuo, support this bill.

A long-term goal of Yeboah's is to complete his education and then get into politics himself. He wants to be elected to **Parliament**, Ghana's governing body, in the next ten years. In Parliament, Yeboah says, "I will try as much as possible to fight for disabled rights and see to it that [disabled citizens] have the same opportunities as the able-bodied people have in the country."[18]

What You Can Do

Yeboah believes that no matter what a person's age or whether or not he or she has a disability, the person can make a difference in the world. If a person wants to get

Emmanuel Yeboah's tireless efforts have caused many Ghanaians to change their views of people with disabilities.

involved with Yeboah's mission to enable the disabled, there are many opportunities. Among the opportunities is to raise funds for the Challenged Athletes Foundation, Free Wheelchair Mission, and Emmanuel's Fund.

To raise money for these organizations, young people can organize fund-raisers such as car washes and bake sales. For example, in 2005 the students at Greenwich Academy's Lower School in Greenwich, Connecticut, raised money for Free Wheelchair Mission by doing chores at home. They donated over $1,000 that they received for their chores.

In addition to fund-raising, young people can volunteer their time to organizations like the Challenged Athletes Foundation and Free Wheelchair Mission. Fifteen-year-old Bryant Schulman of Laguna Beach, California, worked toward his Eagle Scout badge by raising money for thirty wheelchairs for Free Wheelchair Mission in 2005. He also assembled them. He worked with other volunteers to put the wheelchairs together for recipients in Mexico.

Schulman is learning what Emmanuel Yeboah's mother taught him—that with perseverance and determination, anybody can change the world. Although born into poverty and with a disability, Yeboah has already changed how people treat and view Ghana's disabled. "Remarkably, with all his accomplishments, Emmanuel's life is just beginning," states the *Emmanuel's Gift* Web site. "And so too is the impact he will have on a nation—and the world."[19]

Notes

Introduction:
Introducing Emmanuel Ofosu Yeboah
1. Quoted in Ghana Home Page, "Emmanuel Yeboah Preps for Fitness Marathon," July 16, 2005. www.ghanaweb.com/GhanaHome Page/NewsArchive/artikel.php?ID=85911.

Chapter One: A Difficult Start
2. Quoted in CNN, "Life in Baghdad: Emmanuel's Gift," July 15, 2005. http://archives.cnn.com/TRANSCRIPTS/0507/15/lt.01.html.
3. Quoted in Ghana Home Page, "Ghana from Rags to Riches," March 14, 2005. www.ghanaweb.com/GhanaHomePage/NewsArchive/printnews.php?ID=77174.
4. Quoted in *Emmanuel's Gift*, DVD, directed by Lisa Lax and Nancy Stern. Los Angeles, CA: First Look Pictures, 2005.

Chapter Two: Ride of His Life
5. Quoted in Meredy Fullen, "Heroes Take Opportunity for Call to Action," The *O&P Edge*, October 2005. www.oandp.com/edge/issues/articles/2005-10_09.asp.
6. Quoted in Fullen, "Heroes Take Opportunity for Call to Action."

7. Quoted in *Emmanuel's Gift*, "Our Story, His Life." www.emmanuelsgift.com.
8. Quoted in *Emmanuel's Gift*.

Chapter Three: A Vision
9. Quoted in Bob Babbitt, "Interviews with Legends: Emmanuel Ofosu Yeboah," Competitor. www.competitor.com/story. cfm?story_id=11501&pageID=4725.
10. Quoted in *Emmanuel's Gift*.
11. Quoted in Chika Oduah, "Deformity Breeds Strength in Biographical Documentary," *The GSU Signal*, November 15, 2005. www. gsusignal.com/vnews/display.v/ART/2005/11/ 15/437ab00750c11.
12. Quoted in *Emmanuel's Gift*.

Chapter Four: Realizing the Dream
13. Quoted in Oduah, "Deformity Breeds Strength in Biographical Documentary."
14. Quoted in Free Wheelchair Mission, "Travel Log, Ghana," March 2004. www.freewheel chairmission.org/travellog-ghana.html.
15. Emmanuel Yeboah, e-mail message to author, March 13, 2006.

Chapter Five: Emmanuel's Gift
16. Quoted in The Oprah Winfrey Show, "No Excuses," September 29, 2005. www2.

oprah.com/tows/slide/200509/20050929/
slide_20050929_284_209.jhtml.

17. Quoted in Ghana Home Page, "Yeboah Returns Home a Belated Hero," July 28, 2005. www.ghanaweb.com/GhanaHome Page/NewsArchive/artikel.php?ID=86833.
18. Yeboah, e-mail message to author.
19. Quoted in *Emmanuel's Gift*, "Our Story, His Life."

Glossary

activist: A person who uses actions to support a cause.

amputate: To cut off a body part, typically by surgery.

Arthur Ashe Courage Award: An ESPN award presented annually to individuals whose contributions transcend sports.

disabled: Impaired, as in physical functioning.

documentary: A film that presents facts objectively.

handicaps: Physical or mental disabilities.

Parliament: A national representative body having supreme legislative powers within the country.

prostheses: Artificial organs or limbs. The singular form of *prostheses* is *prosthesis*.

For Further Exploration

Books

Terry Cohen and Barry Cohen, *Disabled and Challenged: Reach for Your Dreams!* Clearwater, Florida: WishingUwell Publishing, 2005. Written by Terry Cohen, who, from a young age, learned to accept and conquer the many challenges he faces with myotonic muscular dystrophy and his father, Barry Cohen, a psychologist. This book gives advice to young people who are facing life-long disabilities of all kinds.

Kyle Maynard, *No Excuses: The True Story of a Congenital Amputee Who Became a Champion in Wrestling and in Life.* Washington, DC: Regnery Publishing, 2005. This book is the autobiography of Kyle Maynard who was born without the lower parts of his arms and legs. Maynard excels as a champion athlete, inspirational speaker, college student, and model.

Film

Emmanuel's Gift. DVD. Directed by Lisa Lax and Nancy Stern. Los Angeles, CA: First Look Pictures, 2005. Tells the story of Emmanuel Yeboah's life. The film covers

Yeboah's ride through Ghana, his travels to the United States to bike in races and receive his prosthetic leg, and what he is doing in Ghana to help its disabled citizens.

Web Sites

Challenged Athletes Foundation (www.challenged athletes.org). Web site of CAF, the nonprofit organization that sponsored Emmanuel Yeboah's ride through Ghana. Provides a biography of Yeboah and information about how people can donate to Emmanuel's Fund.

Emmanuel Ofosu Yeboah (www.emmanuelyeboah.org) Yeboah's personal Web site. This Web site includes photos, his biography, and information about donating to his cause.

Emmanuel's Gift (www.emmanuelsgift.com). The official Web site of *Emmanuel's Gift,* the film. Offers information about Emmanuel Yeboah's life story and the production of the documentary. Visitors can view clips of the film.

Free Wheelchair Mission (www.freewheelchairmission.org). Free Wheelchair Mission is the nonprofit organization that partners with Emmanuel Yeboah to provide wheelchairs to Ghana's disabled. This Web site offers information about how people can volunteer for Free Wheelchair Mission.

Index

Picture Credits

About the Author

Leanne K. Currie-McGhee is the author of *Gun Control*, *Animal Rights*, and *Tattoos and Body Piercing*, published by Lucent Books. Ms. Currie-McGhee resides in Norfolk, Virginia, with her husband, Keith, and daughter, Grace.